Anger Management

Taming the Dragon Within

D1738044

Mackenzie Skye, Ph.D., LMFT

Table of Contents

Introduction

I would like to introduce myself. My name is Dr. Mackenzie Skye. I have been practicing in the field of mental health for over 30 years and have helped thousands of clients deal with a variety of mental health challenges they have faced in their lives, and one of the most profound and devastating challenges is in the arena of anger management.

Uncontrolled anger and rage have lasting and devastating effects on individuals, their family members, neighbors, and the community and nation at large.

Anger is an incredibly powerful emotion, and when left unleashed like a roaring, fire-breathing dragon, it can leave in its gigantic tracks a path of destructive, wide-ranging consequences. Uncontrolled anger and rage can impact individuals, families, and even society as a whole. It can cause harm to those around us and lead to legal repercussions that can be incredibly costly.

In this book, we'll explore the topic of anger management, providing insights into the causes and effects of uncontrolled anger, as well as strategies for managing it. We'll examine the impact of uncontrolled anger on individuals, families, and society, discussing the toll it can take on mental and physical health, relationships, and overall well-being.

In addition, we'll examine the legal implications of uncontrolled anger, highlighting the potential legal jeopardy that can result from outbursts of rage and abuse and the impact on financial and social costs of the legal consequences, including the impact on families and communities.

Through a combination of research, real-life case examples, and practical strategies, this book offers a comprehensive guide to anger management. It provides valuable insights and tools for anyone struggling with uncontrolled anger or looking to help someone else who is, and it serves as an important reminder of the power and potential consequences of this complex emotion.

Chapter 1:

Understanding Anger

It's important to know that anger is a natural and powerful emotion that can be experienced by everyone. However, when anger isn't managed properly, it can cause significant harm to ourselves and those around us. The importance of managing anger cannot be overstated, as it can have negative impacts on our physical health, mental health, relationships, and our overall quality of life.

One of the most significant impacts of unmanaged anger is on our physical health. When we experience anger, our body responds with a **"fight, flight, or freeze"** response that triggers a cascade of physiological changes. Our heart rate and blood pressure increase, our breathing becomes faster and shallower, and our muscles tense. While these changes are helpful in situations where we need to defend ourselves, chronic protracted anger can take a huge toll on our bodies.

Case Study

As a licensed mental health practitioner, I had worked with a client we'll call "Ted." Ted was a guy who was always angry about life, from the traffic on his way to work to the weather outside. He was so irritable that he would snap at his coworkers and family members, and no one wanted to be around him.

Over time, Ted's anger began to take a toll on his health. He started experiencing frequent headaches and stomach pains, and he was always tired. His cardiologist had warned him that his stress levels were dangerously high, and he needed to find ways to relax and de-stress.

But from the very beginning of our first meeting, Ted presented as extremely oppositional and refused to change his attitude and behaviors. He believed that being angry was just a part of his personality, and he couldn't imagine living any other way. He wore it as a badge of honor for living his life. He continued to lash out at those around him, even when they tried to help him. He admitted he was a bully but that is how he "got things done."

As time went on, Ted's health deteriorated even further. He developed high blood pressure, which eventually led to his heart attack. He was forced to take time off from work, but he was so consumed by his anger that he couldn't even enjoy the break away from his job. Instead, he spent his days brooding and becoming even more isolated.

Eventually, Ted's health deteriorated to the point where he became disabled. He was unable to work and eventually, he quit. He had to rely on others to take care of him. He filed for disability, but was barely able to live on the monthly stipend he would get. He realized too late that his anger had not only affected his relationships but had also taken a severe toll on his physical and mental health, as well as his finances.

Before he came in for some help and counseling, Ted was left with nothing but regrets. He wished he had listened to the people who had tried to help him earlier in his life, and he wished he had taken better care of his health while he still had the chance. He spent too many years with uncontrolled anger, which had consumed him. He was eventually left by his family along with his regrets. It was going to be a long, slow process for him to recover but at the point he came in seeking support, at least he was willing to learn a new process for him to try and recapture his life while he still had a chance.

The Impacts of Anger

On Ourselves

Research has shown that people who struggle to manage their anger are at higher risk of developing a range of physical health problems, including cardiovascular disease, gastrointestinal problems, and chronic pain. Chronic anger can also weaken our immune system, leaving us more susceptible to illnesses and infections.

In addition to its effects on our physical health, uncontrolled anger can also have significant impacts on our mental health. People who struggle with anger are more likely to experience symptoms of depression, anxiety, and other mental health disorders. They may also have difficulty sleeping, experience increased stress, and have trouble concentrating.

On Our Relationships

Anger can also have negative impacts on our relationships with others. When we lash out in anger or rage, we say or do things that we later regret. This can temporarily, and sometimes even permanently, damage our relationships with friends, family members, and coworkers. Additionally, people who struggle with an inability to control their anger can have trouble maintaining healthy relationships, as their anger can push people to stay away for good.

Case Study

Another client of mine, who we'll call "Maria," was a beautiful young woman who was in love with a man named Jose; they had been together for a couple of years. Jose eventually proposed to Maria and though she said "yes", soon after their engagement plans were announced, their relationship began to deteriorate.

Maria was holding on to a lot of anger inside her; she'd had a difficult, abusive childhood and she often took out her displaced projected frustration and anger on Jose. She would yell at him for small things, criticize him constantly, and would frequently find something to complain or belittle him about. Jose tried his best to be patient and understanding, but her constant picking at him and her misplaced anger towards him was wearing him down.

As time went on, Maria's anger only grew worse. She began to get jealous and possessive, falsely accusing Jose of cheating on her and not spending enough time with her. Jose tried to reassure her that he loved her and would never cheat, but Maria's anger had taken a firm grip on her that wouldn't let go.

Jose eventually couldn't take the stress and anguish of it anymore and he told Maria that he couldn't marry her, and that he needed to end their relationship. Maria was shocked and devastated. She realized that her anger had destroyed the most important relationship in her life. She believed that Jose would always be there for her.

In the aftermath of the breakup, Maria sought help with me for her anger issues. She continued with 1:1 therapy, attended an anger management class, and really started to work on herself. It was a difficult process for her, but Maria eventually learned to control her anger and let go of her past grievances that she had with her abusive father and grieve the relationship that she never had with a father that she had always wanted.

Sometime after their engagement breakup, Maria ran into Jose at a local coffee shop. They caught up with each other and spoke about their past together. Jose told Maria that he was proud of her for getting the help she needed, and that he had forgiven her for the way she had emotionally abused him during their two years together.

Maria realized that even though their relationship had ended, she had learned a valuable lesson about the destructive power of anger and the importance of seeking help when you need it. As Jose began to speak fondly of a warm, engaging woman that he had met after his breakup with Maria and that they were planning to get married, Maria was able to understand that the relationship she could have had with Jose was never to be. It saddened her as she sat there and listened to him over their coffee and silently acknowledged the reality of what a wonderful man Jose was. He deserved the very best and Maria told him so. At that very moment, Maria quietly reaffirmed to herself that learning about anger management and how it had impacted her life would better prepare her going forward with her next relationship, and hopefully it would be with someone as wonderful as Jose.

Techniques to Manage Anger

Fortunately, there are many techniques and strategies that can be used to effectively manage anger. Let's explore these more in depth below.

Identify Triggers

One of the most important strategies is to identify triggers for anger. This may include certain people, situations, or events that tend to trigger anger. Once these triggers are identified, we can work on developing coping strategies to help us manage our anger when we encounter these triggers.

Practice Relaxation Techniques

Another key strategy for managing anger is to practice relaxation techniques. This may include deep breathing, progressive muscle relaxation, or mindfulness meditation. By practicing these techniques regularly, we can learn to calm our bodies and minds when we feel angry, which can help prevent us from reacting impulsively.

Take Cognitive Behavioral Therapy (CBT)

Cognitive-behavioral therapy (CBT) is an effective technique for managing anger. This type of therapy focuses on helping individuals identify and challenge negative thought patterns that contribute to anger. By changing the way we think about situations, we can change the way we feel and react to them. In the last case example, with Maria, she had negative and distorted thought patterns with respect to men in general as well as displaced anger with her father, who had abused her emotionally for most of her life. Sadly but expectedly, she projected those angry, resentful feelings toward Jose, so it was no surprise that their relationship was doomed to fail from the very beginning, since she had never sought treatment or help to change her thinking or feelings about men.

Learn to Communicate Effectively

In addition to these techniques, it's important to practice effective communication skills when we feel angry. This includes learning how to express our feelings in a constructive way, rather than lashing out in anger. By communicating effectively, we can avoid misunderstandings and conflicts that can escalate our anger.

Seek Help

Finally, it's important to seek help when we need it. If anger is causing significant problems in our lives, it may be helpful to seek the support of an anger management group as well as a 1:1 mental health professional. A group can help us through encouragement and support as well as confronting us when we fail to accept ownership of what we do to contribute to dysfunctional communication. They also help us to identify better patterns of communication. Also, seeing a therapist 1:1 can help us identify underlying issues with the use of CBT that may be contributing to our anger, such as in Maria's case, and provide us with tools and strategies to manage it more effectively by learning how CBT works.

Managing anger is a crucial aspect of maintaining our physical and mental health, as well as our relationships with others. By identifying triggers for anger, practicing relaxation techniques, using cognitive-behavioral therapy, practicing effective communication, and seeking help when needed, we can learn to manage our anger more effectively and lead happier, healthier lives. Remember, it's okay to feel angry, but it's important to learn how to express that anger in a constructive way that doesn't harm ourselves or those around us.

Causes and Effects of Anger on a Person

Anger is a powerful emotion that can be experienced by anyone at any time. While it's a natural and healthy emotion, uncontrolled or excessive anger can have a range of negative effects on a person's physical and mental health, relationships, and overall quality of life. Understanding the causes and effects of anger is crucial for learning how to manage this emotion effectively.

Causes of Anger

There are many different causes of anger, ranging from internal factors such as personal beliefs and emotions to external factors such as environmental stressors and interpersonal conflicts. Some of the most common causes of anger include:

- **Personal Beliefs and Emotions:** Personal beliefs and emotions can play a significant role in the experience of anger. For example, if a person has deeply held beliefs about justice or fairness, they may become angry when they perceive or see an injustice or unfairness.

- **Environmental Stressors:** Environmental stressors such as personal finances, inability to pay bills, transportation, being housing insecure, noise, traffic, and crowds can trigger anger in individuals.Similarly, work-related stressors such as long work hours, work dissatisfaction, deadlines, heavy workloads, conflicts with coworkers, and job burnout can also lead to anger.

- **Interpersonal Conflicts:** Conflicts with others, whether they be family members, friends, coworkers, or strangers, can trigger anger in individuals. This may occur when people feel that their needs or values are being ignored or when they feel disrespected, belittled, or unloved.

- **Physical or Emotional Pain:** Physical or emotional pain can also trigger anger in some individuals. For example, a person may become angry if they are in physical pain, if they are experiencing prolonged illness that they have no control over, as well as having other disabilities, experiencing hunger or low blood sugar, or if they are experiencing mental illness such as depression or anxiety. They may be taking medications, or disengaging from addictive substances and are experiencing withdrawal symptoms, which can take a long period of recovery before they are symptom-free.

Effects of Anger

While anger is a natural and healthy emotion, excessive or uncontrolled anger can have a range of negative effects on a person's physical and mental health, as well as their relationships with others. Some of the most common effects of anger include:

- **Physical Health:** Anger can have a range of negative effects on a person's physical health. When a person experiences anger, their body releases stress hormones such as adrenaline and cortisol. Over time, chronic anger can lead to a range of health problems, including high blood pressure, heart disease, and digestive problems.

- **Mental Health:** Excessive or uncontrolled anger can also have negative effects on a person's mental health. People who struggle with anger are more likely to experience symptoms of depression, anxiety, and other mental health disorders. They may also have difficulty sleeping, experience increased stress, and have trouble concentrating.

- **Relationships:** Anger has a significant impact on a person's relationships with others. When a person becomes angry, they say or do things that they later regret. This can alter and damage their relationships with friends, family members, and coworkers. Additionally, people who struggle with anger may have trouble maintaining healthy relationships.

- **Work Performance:** Anger can also have negative effects on a person's work performance. When a person becomes angry at work, they may be more likely to engage in unproductive behaviors such as arguing with coworkers or making mistakes. This can lead to decreased productivity, missed deadlines, and other negative consequences such as termination.

- **Legal Consequences:** In some cases, excessive or uncontrolled anger can lead to legal consequences. For example, a person who becomes violent when they are angry can be arrested and charged with assault or assault and battery, as well as other criminal offenses. They could be issued a restraining order. This has significant long-term consequences, including fines, jail time, and difficulty finding employment or establishing financial security and credit after incarceration.

Benefits of Managing Anger

It's important to discover how to manage anger effectively to avoid the negative consequences associated with excessive or uncontrolled anger.

Effective anger management can have a range of positive benefits for individuals and those around them, which we'll explore below:

1. **Improved Physical Health**

    One of the main benefits of effective anger management is improved physical health. By effectively managing anger, individuals can reduce the negative impact of stress hormones on their body and improve their overall physical health.

2. Better Mental Health

Effective anger management can also have positive effects on a person's mental health. People who struggle with anger are more likely to experience symptoms of depression, anxiety, and other mental health disorders. They may also have difficulty sleeping, they can experience increased stress and cortisol levels in their body, and may have trouble concentrating. Individuals can reduce the negative impact of anger on their mental health and improve their overall well-being.

3. Stronger Relationships

Another significant benefit of effective anger management is stronger relationships. By managing anger effectively, individuals can maintain healthier, more positive connections with others and keep their relationships intact.

4. Improved Work Performance

When a person becomes angry at work, they may be more likely to engage in unproductive behaviors such as arguing with coworkers or making costly mistakes. This can lead to decreased productivity, missed deadlines, and other negative consequences such as termination. By managing anger effectively, individuals can improve their work performance and achieve greater success in their professional lives.

5. Better Decision-Making

When a person is consumed by anger, it can be difficult to think clearly and make rational decisions. Effective anger management can help individuals to regulate their emotions, think more clearly, and make better choices and decisions. This can lead to improved decision-making in all areas of life, from personal relationships to professional endeavors.

6. Increased Self-Awareness

Effective anger management also involves a significant degree of self-awareness. By learning to identify the triggers that cause anger, individuals can gain a better understanding of their emotions and improve their ability to regulate them. This can lead to increased self-awareness and a greater sense of control over one's emotions.

7. Greater Emotional Intelligence

People with high emotional intelligence and awareness can regulate their emotions effectively, identify the emotions of others, and communicate effectively in emotional situations. By developing effective anger management skills, individuals can improve their emotional intelligence and achieve greater success in all areas of life.

8. Improved Communication Skills

Effective anger management also involves the development of strong communication skills. By learning to express emotions in a healthy and productive manner, individuals can improve their ability to communicate with others. This can lead to improved relationships and better decision-making with less conflict and disruption.

9. Increased Resilience

Resilience is the ability to recover quickly from difficult or challenging situations. Developing greater resilience by discovering how to regulate emotions and maintain a positive outlook even in the most difficult circumstance is critical.

Chapter 2:

The Physiology of Anger

Understanding the physiology of anger and the body's response to anger can help individuals to better manage their emotions.

The Body's Response to Anger

Anger is a complex emotion that involves a wide range of physiological responses in the body. When a person becomes angry, their body releases stress hormones such as adrenaline and cortisol. These hormones activate the body's **"fight, flight, or freeze"** response, which prepares the body to respond to a *perceived* or *real* threat.

The body's response to anger can include a wide range of physical sensations, including:

- **Increased Heart Rate:** When a person becomes angry, their heart rate increases as their body prepares to respond to a perceived or real threat. This can lead to feelings of tension and tightness in the chest.

- **Increased Blood Pressure:** Anger can also lead to an increase in blood pressure. This can cause headaches, dizziness, and other physical symptoms.

- **Rapid Breathing:** When a person becomes angry, their breathing may become rapid and shallow. This can lead to feelings of anxiety and panic which can spiral out of control, leading to panic attacks.

- **Sweating:** Anger can also cause sweating as the body works rapidly to regulate its temperature in response to the increased physical activity associated with the fight, flight, or freeze response.

- **Muscle Tension:** Finally, anger can cause muscle tension throughout the body. This can lead to feelings of stiffness, soreness, and discomfort. This can contribute to headaches, neck and back pain.

Effects of Chronic Anger on the Body

During the fight, flight, or freeze response, the body releases a range of hormones, including adrenaline and cortisol. These hormones increase the heart rate, blood pressure, and breathing rate, while also causing the muscles to suddenly tense. This response is designed to help the body.

While the fight, flight, or freeze response can be helpful in certain situations, it can also be harmful if it is activated too often or for too long a period. Chronic anger can lead to a range of negative consequences on a person's physical health, including:

- **Increased Risk of Heart Disease:** This is because the increased heart rate and blood pressure associated with anger can put added strain on the heart, valves and blood vessels.

- **Digestive Problems:** Anger can also lead to digestive problems such as stomachaches, diarrhea, and constipation. This is because the fight, flight, or freeze response can cause the body to redirect blood flow away from the digestive system and toward the muscles and other organs that are needed to respond to either a real or perceived threat.

- **Difficulty Sleeping:** Anger can also make it difficult to sleep. This is because feelings of anxiety and tension interfere with the body's ability to fully relax and fall asleep.

- **Weakened Immune System:** Chronic anger can also weaken the immune system, making it more difficult for the body to fight off infections and illnesses. This is because the stress hormones released during the fight, flight, or freeze response can interfere with the body's natural immune response system.

Effects of Chronic Anger on the Mind

Chronic anger and stress can also lead to negative consequences for a person's mental health, including:

- **Increased Risk of Mental Health Disorders:** Chronic anger can increase the risk of mental health problems such as depression and anxiety as well as panic attacks and post-traumatic stress disorder (PTSD). This is because the stress hormones released during the fight, flight, or freeze response can interfere with the body's natural stress response system.

- **Decreased Self-Esteem:** Anger can also lead to decreased self-esteem, as a person may feel guilty or ashamed of their outburst of anger whether it is in private or public. This can contribute to negative mental health outcomes, including depression and anxiety.

- **Interpersonal Problems:** Anger can also lead to interpersonal problems, as a person may lash out at others or become aggressive in response to perceived threats. This can permanently alter relationships and contributes to feelings of isolation, loneliness, depression, and anxiety.

Tools for Managing Anger at Home

The following are effective tools you can use to help manage your anger:

- **Recognize Your Triggers**

  The first step in managing anger effectively is to recognize the triggers that cause anger. This can involve keeping a "bullet journal" to track what situations or events tend to cause anger. This can be done by simply writing down a few words (bullet points) about what started or created the trigger for you.

- **Engage in Physical Activity**

  Engaging in regular physical activity can also help to reduce feelings of stress and tension, as well as improve overall physical health. Exercise is a great way to manage the physical symptoms of anger, as it can help to reduce muscle tension and promote relaxation. Exercise can also release endorphins, which are natural mood-boosting chemicals in the brain that can help to reduce feelings of stress and tension.

  To incorporate exercise into your anger management routine, try to engage in at least 20 minutes of moderate-intensity exercise on most days of the week, as long as your health provider acknowledges the safety of doing exercise for you. This can include activities such as brisk walking, jogging, swimming, or cycling. If you are new to exercise, start slowly and gradually increase the duration and intensity of your workouts over time.

- **Practice Relaxation Techniques**

  Practicing daily relaxation techniques such as deep breathing, meditation, and yoga can help to regulate emotions and reduce feelings of stress and tension.

Daily Relaxation Techniques

Here are some relaxation techniques you can incorporate into your daily life to help manage anger and stress.

- **Deep Breathing**

  Deep breathing is a simple and effective technique for managing the physical symptoms of anger. When a person becomes angry, their breathing tends to become shallow and rapid, which can contribute to feelings of tension and stress. Deep breathing involves taking slow, deep breaths, which can help to slow the heart rate, reduce blood pressure, and promote relaxation.

  To practice deep breathing:

1. Find a quiet and comfortable place to sit or lie down.

2. Close your eyes and take a deep breath in through your nose, filling your lungs with air.

3. Hold the breath for a few seconds.

4. Slowly exhale through your mouth, letting the air out completely.

5. Repeat this process for a few minutes, focusing on the sensation of the breath smoothly moving in and out of your body.

- **Progressive Muscle Relaxation**

  Progressive muscle relaxation is a technique that involves tensing and then relaxing different muscle groups throughout the body. This can help to reduce muscle tension and promote relaxation, which can help to manage the physical symptoms of anger.

  To practice progressive muscle relaxation:

1. Find a quiet and comfortable place to sit or lie down.

2. Start by tensing the muscles in your toes and feet.

3. Hold the tension for a few seconds.

4. Release the tension and allow the muscles to relax completely.

5. Move up to the muscles in your calves and thighs.

6. Repeat the process of tensing and relaxing.

7. Continue this process, moving up through the muscles in your abdomen, chest, back, arms, and neck, until you have tensed and relaxed every muscle group in your body including your eyes, eyebrows, and jaw.

- **Mindfulness Meditation**

  Mindfulness meditation is a technique that involves focusing your attention on the present moment, without judgment or distraction. This can help to reduce feelings of stress and tension, as well as promote relaxation and a sense of calm.

  To practice mindfulness meditation:

1. Find a quiet and comfortable place to sit or lie down.

2. Close your eyes and focus your attention on your breath.

3. Allow your thoughts and emotions to come and go without judgment or distraction.

4. If your mind wanders, gently bring your attention back to your breath.

  Start with just a few minutes of meditation each day, gradually increasing the duration over time.

- **Visualization**

  Visualization is a technique that involves creating a mental image of a peaceful and calming scene. This can help to reduce feelings of stress and tension, as well as promote relaxation and a sense of calm.

  To practice visualization:

1. Find a quiet and comfortable place to sit or lie down.

2. Close your eyes and imagine a peaceful and calming scene, such as a quiet beach, a tranquil forest, or a serene mountain lake.

3. Use all your senses to gather your image.

4. Reflect on your visualization scene quietly for at least 5 minutes.

Let me share my own visual image that helps me every single time I need to conjure it up. It goes like this:

At the time, I was in my twenties and I was with my grandmother Nina, who I loved dearly. We are walking hand in hand along the warm waters of the northern gulf shore of Florida in Dunedin, where she lived a couple of blocks away. We are both walking barefoot. She is in a pretty short-sleeved pink dress with her pretty pearl necklace that she often would wear to church, and I am in a t-shirt and shorts. I remember our feet feeling the warm sand. We see and hear the squawking seagulls flying high over our heads. There are just a few people on the beach, it is quiet, and the sky is wide open and blue. We can hear the gentle sounds of the waves lapping at the shoreline. Along the white-sugar-sand beach as we walk hand in hand, we are looking for giant Conch shells and my grandmother soon spots one. We both walk over to explore it and my grandmother picks it up gently from where it was resting, dusting off the sand with her old, wrinkled, arthritic hands, and then holds it up to her ear. My grandmother then says to me in her southern drawl while she is holding the shell to her ear, "Can you hear that, honey? It's God's breath!" She places it slowly to my ear and I hear the gentle air rush through the Conch shell and sure enough, I do believe I hear Him! The feelings that I experience at that captured moment in time is one of absolute pure joy, love, and safety all at once. It brings tears to our eyes and my grandmother's beautiful, big, blue eyes just sparkle like the sun dancing on that big, beautiful ocean as we stand on the white-sugar-like sands of the gulf shore, experiencing that precious lingering moment together. I love and cherish that memory. Nina has been gone for many years now, but she lives lovingly in my heart, so she is with me everywhere I go. But when I need a visual image to help me, Nina is always there with me on that beach those many years ago, saying, "Can you hear that, honey? It's God's breath!"

When to Seek Professional Help

If anger is having a significant impact on a person's physical or mental health, it is helpful to seek professional help. This may involve working with a therapist or counselor to develop strategies for managing anger as well as participating in an anger management class or therapy group. An ideal sized group is 6-8 participants.

There are other factors one should be aware of when one is seeking the help of a mental health practitioner when dealing with either court ordered anger management classes or when ordered to participate in anger management as a result of acts of domestic violence or child abuse and in extreme cases, when one has expressed to a licensed mental health practitioner their intention to commit homicide and they have a weapon of lethality and an identified victim. This information when conveyed of either engaging in or their intent to engage in domestic violence, child abuse, elder abuse or homicidal intention are not protected, and the therapist is required by law to breach confidentiality and report to law enforcement.

Chapter 3:

Identifying Emotional Triggers

Everyone experiences emotions, and it's natural to react to different situations in different ways. However, certain events or situations can trigger intense emotional responses, which can be difficult to manage. Identifying emotional triggers is the first step in learning how to manage these responses effectively. Next, we'll explore what emotional triggers are and provide some tips for identifying personal triggers for anger.

What Are Emotional Triggers?

Emotional triggers are events or situations that elicit strong emotional responses, such as anger, sadness, fear, or anxiety. These triggers can be internal or external, and they are unique to everyone. For example, some people may become angry when they feel disrespected, while others may become anxious when they are in large crowds.

Identifying emotional triggers is important because it allows a person to better understand their emotional responses and learn how to manage them effectively. Once a person is aware of their triggers, they can take steps to avoid or manage them when they arise.

How to Identify Personal Triggers for Anger

Anger is a common emotional response, and identifying personal triggers for anger is crucial for managing this emotion effectively. Here are some tips for identifying personal triggers for anger:

- **Keep a Journal**

  One way to identify personal triggers for anger is to keep a journal of your emotional responses. Whenever you feel angry, try and jot down the situation that triggered the response, your thoughts and feelings in the moment, and any physical sensations you experienced. After a few weeks or months of journaling, look back at your entries and look for patterns or common themes in the situations that triggered your anger.

- **Reflect on Past Experiences**

  Reflecting on your past experiences can also help to identify personal triggers for anger. Think about situations in your past when you have felt angry and try to identify what triggered the response.

  Ask yourself questions such as:

  What was happening in the situation before I got angry?

  _____
  _____
  _____
  _____
  _____
  _____
  _____
  _____

  What thoughts or feelings did I have at the moment?

  _____
  _____
  _____
  _____
  _____

_____

_____

_____

What physical sensations did I experience? (For example, you may have felt your blood pressure rise, got hot in the face, shook, trembled, began to sweat, felt dizzy, or noticed a dry mouth, red eyes, or shallow breathing.)

_____

_____

_____

_____

_____

_____

_____

What was my physical response to this trigger? (For example, your voice may have increased in volume; you may have experienced a flushed face, tense muscles, rapid heartbeat, or shallow, quick breaths; you may have pointed a finger or a fist, slammed a door or something else with your hand, threw or broke something, yelled or screamed, or walked or sped away quickly and recklessly in a car; or you may have sought drugs and/or alcohol.)

_____

_____

_____

_____

_____

_____

_____

_____

How long did it take for you to regain your composure and return to your "norm?" (For example, 5, 10, 15, 20, 30, 45 minutes, or 1, 2, 4, 8, 24 hours.)

_____
_____
_____
_____
_____
_____
_____
_____

On a scale from 1 to 10 with 10 being the most significant, how high was this score for this anger event and why was that?

_____
_____
_____
_____
_____
_____
_____
_____

- **Pay Attention to Your Physical Responses**

When you become angry, pay attention to your physical responses and by doing this, it can help you identify personal triggers for anger. For example, if you notice that you always become angry when you feel tense or agitated, this could be a personal trigger for your anger.

What are your physical symptoms you notice at the precise moment you begin to get angry?

_____

_____

_____

_____

_____

_____

_____

_____

_____

- **Notice Your Thought Patterns**

  Our thoughts often contribute to our emotional responses, and noticing our thought patterns can help to identify personal triggers for anger. Pay attention to the thoughts you have when you feel angry and try to identify any negative or distorted thought patterns that may be contributing to the response. For example, if you always become angry when someone disagrees with you, you may have a belief that your opinions are always right, which is contributing to the response and sets up a discord of always having a win-or-lose attitude, which is unhealthy. Aim for win-win solutions. Keep it on balance. No one likes to lose. Compromise whenever you can, as it feels really good when you do.

  What are the most recurring thoughts you have just before you notice you get angry and is there a pattern?

_____

_____

_____

_____

_____

_____

_____

_____

- **Seek Feedback From Others**

  Sometimes it can be difficult to identify personal triggers for anger on our own. Seeking feedback from trusted friends or family members can help to provide insight into our emotional responses. Ask them to share their observations of situations where you have become angry and what they think may have triggered the response.

  What are they observing about you when you get angry and what is their feedback to you?

  _____

  _____

  _____

  _____

  _____

  _____

  _____

  _____

  Remember when they give you feedback, it is not your time to debate what they are observing or reporting to you. Just listen and absorb what they are saying to you. Thank them and reflect. Be silent, do not engage with them or attempt to argue what they have observed about you.

Managing Personal Triggers for Anger

Once personal triggers for anger have been identified, it's important to develop strategies for managing them effectively. Here are some tips for managing personal triggers for anger:

- **Avoid Triggers When Possible**

  Avoiding triggers when possible is one of the most effective ways to manage personal triggers for anger. For example, if you know that you become angry when you are in a crowded environment, you may choose to avoid large social gatherings or take breaks when you feel overwhelmed.

  How can I avoid my triggers? (For example, take a step back, take a break, walk away, change the subject, shorten the time you spend with someone that you know is a trigger, give yourself time to breathe deeply, go for a quick walk, visualize, or meditate.)

  1. _____
     _____
     _____

  2. _____
     _____
     _____

  3. _____
     _____
     _____

  4. _____
     _____
     _____

  5. _____
     _____
     _____

- **Develop Coping Strategies**

  Developing coping strategies for managing anger triggers involves identifying the triggers and developing a plan for how to respond to them. Here are some steps to take to develop coping strategies:

1. Identify Your Triggers

The first step in developing coping strategies is to identify your triggers. This involves understanding the situations or events that trigger your anger. It may be helpful to keep a journal or log of the situations that trigger your anger and the emotions and physical sensations you experience in response to them. Identify your triggers below:

1. _____
   _____
   _____

2. _____
   _____
   _____

3. _____
   _____
   _____

4. _____
   _____
   _____

5. _____
   _____
   _____

2. Recognize the Signs of Anger

Once you have identified your triggers, it's important to recognize the signs of anger. This may include physical sensations such as a racing heart or muscle tension, as well as emotional responses such as irritability or frustration.

What are your physical signs of anger?

1. _____

_____

_____

2. _____

_____

_____

3. _____

_____

_____

4. _____

_____

_____

5. _____

_____

_____

3. Practice Relation Techniques

Relaxation techniques such as deep breathing, progressive muscle relaxation, and meditation can help to reduce feelings of anger and promote a sense of calmness. Practicing these techniques regularly can help you to manage your anger triggers more effectively.

What is a healthy way for you to relax?

_____

_____

_____

_____

_____

_____

_____

_____

_____

4. Develop a Plan for How to Respond

Develop a plan for how to respond to your triggers. This may involve using relaxation techniques, practicing mindfulness, or engaging in physical activity to release pent-up energy.

Write down what your plan will be here: (For example, slow down your breathing, take 5 deep breaths, take a physical step back, redirect your attention for 5 minutes, be quiet, be still, go for a walk, listen to soothing environmental sounds, visualize, meditate, count to 100, or use progressive muscle relaxation).

_____

_____

_____

_____

_____

_____

_____

_____

_____

5. Seek Support

If you are having difficulty managing your anger triggers, it may be helpful to seek support from a mental health professional. A therapist and an anger management group can work with you to identify your triggers, develop coping strategies, and provide support as you begin to work to manage your anger and learn new coping strategies.

Examples of Coping Strategies for Managing Anger Triggers

1. Deep Breathing

Taking slow, deep breaths can help to promote a sense of calm. Inhale deeply through your nose, hold the breath for a few seconds, and then exhale slowly through your mouth.

2. Progressive Muscle Relaxation

Progressive muscle relaxation involves tensing and relaxing different muscle groups in your body to release tension and reduce feelings of anger. Start by tensing the muscles in your feet and then releasing them, and then work your way up your body to your head.

3. Mindfulness

Practicing mindfulness involves being present in the moment and focusing on your thoughts and feelings without judgment. This can help to promote a sense of calm. Try focusing on your breath or a specific object and bring your attention back to it whenever your mind begins to wander.

4. Engaging in Physical Activity

Engaging in physical activity such as walking, running, dancing, working out, or lifting weights can help to release pent-up energy. Choose an activity that you enjoy and that allows you to release tension in a healthy way. The creative arts, such as painting, clay-work, sculpting, and glassmaking, can also be of great value.

Chapter 4:

Coping Strategies

Coping strategies for managing anger triggers involves identifying the triggers, recognizing the signs of anger, practicing relaxation techniques, developing a plan for how to respond, and seeking support when necessary. By developing coping strategies, you can learn to manage your anger more effectively and reduce the negative impact that anger can have on your life.

Common Triggers for Anger

While some people may experience anger more frequently than others, there are certain triggers that are common among most people. In the following, we'll explore the most common triggers for anger.

- **Frustration:** When we feel frustrated, we often feel as though we are not able to accomplish what we want or need to do. This can be due to external factors such as obstacles or challenges, or internal factors such as self-doubt or low self-esteem.

- **Injustice:** When we feel as though we have been wronged or treated unfairly, we may become angry. This can be due to situations such as being mistreated at work or experiencing discrimination based on race, gender, or other factors.

- **Disrespect:** When we feel as though we are not being treated with the respect that we deserve, we may become angry. This can be due to situations such as being dismissed, demeaned, being ignored, or having our opinions diminished or cast aside.

- **Threats:** When we feel as though our safety or well-being is being threatened, we may become angry. This can be due to situations such as being verbally or physically threatened by someone else.

- **Negative Memories:** When we are reminded of past negative experiences or traumas, we may become angry. This can be due to situations such as encountering a person or place that is associated with a negative memory.

- **Loss of Control:** When we feel as though we are not in control of a situation, we may become angry. This can be due to situations such as being stuck in traffic, when driving behind a slow driver, or experiencing a loss of power or control in a personal or professional situation.

- **Betrayal:** When we feel as though someone has violated our trust or betrayed us in some way, we become angry and hurt. This can be due to situations such as being lied to or cheated on by a friend or a loved one. There is an old saying that a friend once told me: "All people will disappoint you." The lesson here is no one can meet all your expectations over the course of your life. Forgiveness is a blessing that we must all learn to live by, but it sure isn't easy.

Case Study

I worked with someone who had been incarcerated (We'll call him "John") at one of the state prisons and who had been married to his wife ("Sarah") for over a decade. They had built a life together, with a beautiful house, a nice car, and a sizable bank account. However, things were not as perfect as they seemed.

John began to suspect that Sarah was having an affair, but he tried to ignore his gut feelings and gave her the benefit of the doubt. However, as time went on, his suspicions grew stronger and he started to investigate. To his horror, he found out that Sarah had been cheating on him with his best friend.

John was devastated by this betrayal. He felt like his entire world had crumbled around him, and his anger began to build up inside him like a volcano ready to erupt. He confronted Sarah and his friend, and they admitted to their affair.

Unable to control his emotions, John spiraled out of control. He became consumed with rage and decided to take revenge on his unfaithful wife and best friend. He burned down their house, destroyed her car, and emptied out their bank accounts.

As the flames engulfed their home, John stood there in a daze, watching everything he and his wife had worked for go up in flames. It wasn't until the police arrived that he realized the magnitude of what he had done.

John was arrested and later charged with arson and theft. He spent several years in prison, isolated from the world and left with only his regret and anger to keep him company.

At the end of his incarceration, John realized that his actions had only hurt himself and those around him. He never forgot the pain of the betrayal, but over a long-protracted period of time, he learned how to manage his anger and to move on with his life.

- **Personal Insults:** When we feel as though someone has insulted us or attacked us personally, we may become bitter and angry. This can be due to situations such as being called names or being corrected or belittled in front of others.

Case Study

Another client I worked with ("Jack") had been married to "Alice" for over 25 years, and during that time, Jack had developed a habit of correcting Alice in front of others. At first, Alice brushed it off, but as time went on, it became more and more frequent, and Alice began to feel humiliated, demeaned and hurt by it.

Despite numerous requests from Alice over the years they were together to stop correcting her in public, Jack continued to do so, completely oblivious and unaware of how much it was hurting and humiliating her as well as affecting her self-esteem. Alice tried to talk to him about it, but he always brushed it off, telling her that she was overreacting and that she was just too sensitive or that he was just joking with her.

As the years went by, Alice began to feel increasingly isolated and alone. She stopped wanting to go out with Jack to social events, knowing that he would inevitably correct her in front of others. She frequently felt like she was walking on eggshells around him, afraid to say or do anything that might provoke his criticism with her. She had become drained and exhausted.

Finally, after years of feeling miserable and unhappy, and after one more episode of public correction and humiliation, Alice decided that she had had enough. She packed her bags and moved out of their home, leaving Jack behind. For a long time, Jack was unable to understand why Alice had left him, as he knew that she loved him. He refused to see how his behavior had been so hurtful and how it could warrant her leaving him.

As time went on, Jack began to realize the extent of his mistakes. He started to understand just how much his constant correcting had hurt Alice, and he regretted not listening to her sooner. He tried to reach out to her, but she was still too hurt to want to speak to him.

Time went by and Jack remained alone, filled with regret for the way he had treated Alice. Finally, one day Jack received a letter from her. In it, Alice explained that she had moved on with her life and found happiness with someone else. She forgave Jack for his past mistakes over their long marriage together but made it clear that she had absolutely no interest in rekindling their relationship ever again. Too much water had gone over the bridge over too many years. The damage was done.

As Jack slowly read the letter, he felt a deep sense of sadness and regret wash over him. He realized that he had lost the love of his life because of his own selfishness and inability to listen to her needs and to be accountable for his abusive actions toward her. From that day on, he vowed to gain better communication skills with others and listen with kindness and respect, never again making the same mistake he had with Alice.

The Link Between Thoughts, Feelings, and Behaviors

Have you ever wondered why you sometimes feel certain emotions or behave in certain ways without fully understanding why? The answer lies in the complex relationship between thoughts, feelings, and behaviors. Let's explore this link next.

- **Thoughts** are the internal narrative we have about the world around us. They can be conscious or unconscious and can have a powerful influence on our emotions and behavior. For example, if you are in a stressful situation, your thoughts may be focused on the negative aspects of the situation, leading to feelings of anxiety or fear. On the other hand, if you are in a positive situation, your thoughts may be focused on the positive aspects, leading to feelings of happiness or contentment.

- **Feelings** are our emotional responses to the world around us. They can be influenced by our thoughts, past experiences, and physical sensations. For example, if you have a negative thought about a situation, you may experience feelings of sadness or anger. Conversely, if you have a positive thought about a situation, you may experience feelings of joy or excitement.

- **Behaviors** are the actions we take in response to our thoughts and feelings. They can be conscious or unconscious and can have a powerful impact on our mental health and well-being. For example, if you are feeling stressed, you may engage in behaviors such as smoking or overeating to cope with your emotions. Alternatively, if you are feeling happy, you may engage in behaviors such as exercise or spending time with loved ones to enhance your mood.

The link between thoughts, feelings, and behaviors is complex and multifaceted. Our thoughts influence our feelings, which in turn influence our behaviors. However, the relationship is not one-way. Our behaviors can also influence our thoughts and feelings. For example, engaging in activities that bring us joy can lead to positive thoughts and feelings.

This link can be both positive and negative. Negative thoughts can lead to negative feelings and behaviors, while positive thoughts can lead to positive feelings and behaviors. Understanding this link can help you better manage your mental health by identifying and challenging negative thoughts and behaviors.

For example, if you are experiencing feelings of anxiety, you may identify the negative thoughts that are contributing to your emotions. You may then challenge these thoughts by examining and looking for the evidence for and against the thoughts that you hold to believe. By challenging negative thoughts, you can then begin to change your feelings and behaviors, as faulty or distorted beliefs serve you no positive purpose and are destructive to your well-being. But the trick is doing it at the moment they appear. You can change them midstream at the very moment they surface. You essentially redirect yourself quickly to having a positive thought or reframing the outcome. This is what is referred to as CBT, Cognitive Behavioral Therapy.

Similarly, if you are engaging in behaviors that are harmful to your mental health, you may identify the thoughts and feelings that are driving your actions and behaviors. By examining these thoughts and feelings, you can develop alternative strategies for a different behavioral outcome.

In conclusion, the link between thoughts, feelings, and behaviors is complex and multifaceted. Understanding this link can help you better manage your mental health by identifying and challenging negative thoughts and behaviors. By doing so, you can change your feelings and behaviors, leading to more positive results.

Cognitive Restructuring using CBT Cognitive Behavioral Therapy

Cognitive-behavioral therapy (CBT) is a widely used approach for managing anger which involves using the strategies outlined below:

1. **Recognizing and challenging negative thoughts:** Negative thoughts can contribute to feelings of anger. Cognitive-behavioral therapy helps you to recognize and challenge these thoughts, replacing them with more positive and realistic thoughts. This can help you to feel less angry and more in control.

2. **Developing coping strategies:** Coping strategies are the techniques and behaviors that you use to manage your anger. As we have discussed before, these can include relaxation techniques, deep breathing or meditation, or activities that help you to feel calmer, such as exercise or spending time in nature.

3. **Practicing problem-solving skills:** Sometimes anger can arise from feeling helpless in a situation. Cognitive-behavioral therapy can help you to develop problem-solving skills, so that you can take control of the situation and feel more empowered.

Which coping strategies for managing anger will you use? Check them off as you read!

- **Take a time-out:** When you feel yourself becoming overwhelmed with anger, take a time-out. Remove yourself from the situation and take a break, whether that means going for a walk, listening to music, or doing something else that helps you to relax.

- **Use relaxation techniques:** Relaxation techniques such as deep breathing, meditation, or progressive muscle relaxation can help to reduce feelings of anger and promote relaxation.

- **Engage in physical activity:** Exercise is a great way to reduce feelings of anger and stress. Engaging in physical activity can help promote feelings of relaxation.

- **Use CBT Cognitive Behavioral Therapy strategies:** Cognitive-behavioral strategies, such as recognizing and challenging negative thoughts, can help to reduce feelings of anger and promote positive thinking.

- **Seek support:** Talking to a friend or family member, or seeking the help of a therapist, can be a helpful way to manage feelings of anger. Talking about your feelings can help you to feel heard and validated, and can help you to gain perspective on the situation.

CBT Cognitive Behavioral Therapy can be an effective approach for managing anger. By identifying triggers, recognizing and challenging negative thoughts, and developing coping strategies, you can learn to manage your anger in a healthy and productive way. Coping strategies such as taking a time-out, using relaxation techniques, engaging in physical activity, using cognitive-behavioral strategies, and seeking support can all be helpful ways to manage feelings of anger. With practice and perseverance, you can learn to manage your anger in a way that promotes positive mental health and well-being.

More Coping Techniques for Anger Management

Relaxation Techniques

Relaxation techniques are a great way to reduce feelings of anger and promote relaxation. Here are some creative relaxation techniques that you can use to reduce anger:

Which ones will you use?

- **Visualization** is a powerful relaxation technique that involves imagining a peaceful and calming scene. Close your eyes and imagine yourself in a beautiful and tranquil environment, such as a beach or a forest. Imagine the sounds, smells, and sensations of this environment, and focus on your breathing as you visualize yourself becoming calmer and more relaxed.

- **Progressive muscle relaxation** starts by tensing the muscles in your feet and then releasing the tension, moving up to your calves, thighs, and so on until you have tensed and relaxed every muscle group in your body.

- **Aromatherapy** involves using essential oils to promote relaxation and reduce stress. Lavender, chamomile, and peppermint are all great essential oils for reducing anger and promoting relaxation. You can diffuse these oils in a diffuser, add them to a warm bath, or apply them topically. I personally love the scent of lavender that I use every night before bedtime.

- **Yoga** is a great way to promote relaxation and reduce stress. Practicing yoga can help you to become more aware of your body and your breath, promoting a sense of calm and relaxation.

- **Coloring** (and other fine arts) is a creative and relaxing activity that can help to reduce feelings of anger and stress. You can purchase adult coloring books, or print out coloring pages from the internet, and spend time coloring in intricate designs and patterns.

- **Listening to calming music** can help to reduce feelings of anger and promote relaxation. Choose music that you find soothing and calming, and listen to it in a quiet and comfortable environment.

- **Progressive environmental sounds** are sounds that gradually become more soothing and relaxing, such as the sound of a waterfall or waves crashing on the shore. You can find progressive relaxation sounds on YouTube or other websites, and listen to them as you practice deep breathing or other relaxation techniques.

There are numerous creative relaxation techniques that you can use to reduce feelings of anger and promote relaxation. Visualization, progressive muscle relaxation, aromatherapy, yoga, coloring, listening to music, and progressive relaxation sounds are all great techniques for reducing anger and promoting relaxation. Experiment with different techniques to find the ones that work best for you, and make relaxation a regular part of your routine to promote positive mental health and well-being. I personally have a sound machine that I use on my nightstand and I love the sound of crickets singing away to each other, along with the sound of soft gentle summer breezes.

Mindfulness and Meditation Techniques

Mindfulness and meditation are powerful techniques for managing anger and promoting emotional well-being. By practicing mindfulness and meditation regularly, you can develop greater awareness of your thoughts and feelings, and learn to respond to them in a more calm and constructive way. In this section, we'll explore some of the key techniques and benefits of mindfulness and meditation for anger management.

What Is Mindfulness?

Mindfulness is the practice of being present in the moment, without judgment or distraction. It involves focusing your attention on your breath, your body, and your surroundings, and becoming aware of your thoughts and feelings without becoming overwhelmed by them. By practicing mindfulness regularly, you can develop greater clarity, focus, and emotional resilience, which can help you to manage your anger more effectively.

What can you be mindful of in the quiet of your moment?

_____

_____

_____

_____

_____

_____

_____

What Is Meditation?

Meditation is a form of mindfulness practice that involves sitting quietly and focusing your attention on your breath or a specific object, such as a candle or a mantra. By meditating regularly, you can develop greater calmness and clarity of mind, which can help you to manage your anger more quickly and effectively. Here are some meditation techniques that you can use for anger management:

Which ones will you try? Check them off as you go.

- **Breath awareness meditation:** This involves focusing your attention on your breath, noticing the sensations of air moving in and out of your body, and allowing your thoughts and feelings to come and go without judgment or distraction.

- **Body scan meditation:** This involves scanning your body from head to toe, noticing any areas of tension or discomfort, and releasing it through focused breathing and relaxation.

- **Loving-kindness meditation:** This involves sending feelings of love, compassion, and kindness to yourself and others, including those who may have caused you harm or frustration in the past.

- **Mantra meditation:** This involves repeating a word or phrase, such as "peace" or "calm," to help focus your mind and reduce stress and tension.

Benefits of Mindfulness and Meditation for Anger Management

Mindfulness and meditation offer many benefits for managing anger and promoting emotional well-being, including:

- **Increased self-awareness:** Mindfulness and meditation can help you become more aware of your thoughts, feelings, and physical sensations, which can help you identify and manage your anger triggers more effectively.

- **Reduced stress and anxiety:** Practicing mindfulness and meditation helps to reduce stress and anxiety, preventing feelings of anger from escalating.

- **Improved emotional regulation:** By practicing mindfulness and meditation, you can learn to respond to your thoughts and feelings in a more calm and constructive way, which can help you manage your anger more effectively.

- **Greater empathy and compassion:** Mindfulness and meditation can help you to develop greater empathy and compassion for yourself and others, which can help to reduce feelings of anger and promote more positive relationships.

Experiment with different mindfulness and meditation techniques to find the ones that work best for you, and make them a regular part of your self-care routine. I personally enjoy the app CALM, which really helps to guide me at night before I go to sleep.

Chapter 5:

Communication and Conflict

Resolution

Effective communication and conflict resolution are key skills for managing anger and promoting healthy relationships. When we feel angry, it can be difficult to express ourselves in a clear and constructive way, which can lead to misunderstandings and further conflict. In this next area, we'll explore some effective communication techniques for expressing anger and resolving conflicts constructively.

What Is Effective Communication?

Effective communication involves expressing yourself clearly and respectfully and listening actively to others. When communicating effectively, you're able to express your thoughts, feelings, and needs in a way that is assertive but not aggressive, and you're able to listen to others with empathy and respect. Effective communication is an essential skill for managing anger and resolving conflicts, as it allows you to express your feelings and needs constructively, and to understand and respect the feelings and needs of others.

What Is Conflict Resolution?

Conflict resolution is resolving conflicts constructively, through open communication, empathy, and problem-solving. Conflict can arise in any relationship, and when managed effectively, can lead to deeper understanding and stronger connections. People must manage conflict effectively to avoid escalating into anger, resentment, and further conflict. Conflict resolution involves actively listening to the perspectives of others, expressing your own perspective in a clear and respectful way, and working together to find solutions that meet the needs of everyone involved.

Effective Techniques for Expressing Anger

When we feel angry, it can be difficult to express ourselves in a clear and constructive way. Here are some effective communication techniques for expressing anger in a way that is assertive but not aggressive:

- **Use "I" statements**

  When expressing anger, it's important to use "I" statements, such as "I feel frustrated when..." or "I need..." This helps to communicate your feelings and needs in a clear and assertive way, without placing blame on others.

I feel

_____

I need

_____.

- **Express empathy**

  When expressing anger, it's important to also express empathy for the other person's perspective. This can help to defuse defensiveness and promote a more constructive dialogue. For example, you could say, "I understand you were trying to help, but I feel frustrated when you interrupt me." Fill in below.

I understand that you were

_____

but I feel _____when you _____.

- **Take a break**

  If you feel overwhelmed with anger, it's okay to take a break and come back to the conversation when you are feeling calmer. This can help to prevent the situation from escalating into further conflict.

- **Avoid blaming and accusing**

  When expressing anger, it's important to avoid blaming and accusing others, as this can lead to defensiveness and further conflict. Instead, focus on expressing your own feelings and needs in a clear and respectful way.

- **Listen actively**

  When communicating with others, it's important to listen actively, and to understand their perspective. This can help to build empathy and promote a more constructive dialogue.

- **Find common ground**

  When resolving conflicts, it's important to look for common ground, and to focus on finding solutions that meet the needs of everyone involved. This can help to promote a more collaborative and constructive approach.

- **Brainstorm solutions**

  When resolving conflicts, it can be helpful to brainstorm different solutions, and to evaluate each solution based on its feasibility and effectiveness. This can be extremely helpful when trying to resolve conflicts.

Effective Techniques for Resolving Conflicts

Resolving conflicts in a healthy way can be challenging, especially in the moment when you are feeling angry. However, there are several key strategies that can help you resolve conflicts in a way that promotes understanding and strengthens relationships, rather than causing further damage. Some of these techniques are the same ones used for expressing anger, but they bear repeating, as they apply to both situations.

- **Take a deep breath and calm down**

  When you're feeling angry, it's important to take a step back and calm down before you try to resolve a conflict. Take a few deep breaths and try to relax your body. This will help you think more clearly and approach the situation with a level head.

- **Use "I" statements**

  When expressing your feelings about a conflict, it's important to use "I" statements rather than "you" statements. This helps to avoid placing blame and promotes a more constructive conversation. For example, instead of saying "You never listen to me," you could say "I feel like my concerns aren't being heard".

- **Listen actively!**

- Active listening is an important part of resolving conflicts in a healthy way. When someone is speaking to you, try to really hear what they're saying without interrupting or formulating a response. Ask clarifying questions if necessary to make sure you understand their perspective.

- **Empathize with the other person**

  Empathy is the ability to understand and share the feelings of another person. When you're in a conflict, it's important to try to empathize with the other person's perspective, even if you don't agree with it. This can help you find common ground and work toward a solution together.

- **Focus on the issue, not the person**

  When resolving a conflict, it's important to focus on the issue at hand rather than attacking the other person's character. This helps to keep the conversation constructive and avoids escalating the conflict. Stick to the facts and avoid making assumptions or generalizations.

- **Brainstorm solutions together**

  Once you've both had a chance to express your perspectives, it's time to work together to find a solution that works for everyone. Brainstorm ideas and be open to compromise. Remember that the goal is to find a solution that everyone can live with, not necessarily one that satisfies everyone completely.

- **Agree on next steps**

  Once you've come up with a solution, make sure to agree on the next steps. This might involve putting the solution into action or setting up a plan for follow-up. After a conflict has been resolved, it's important to follow up to ensure that the resolution has been successful. This can help to build trust and prevent future conflicts.

Here are some examples of follow-up conversations:

1. So we can agree that

    _____?

2. Let's follow up with each other at the end of the day to see how we are doing, okay?

3. Let's check in with each other in the future to make sure the conflict doesn't resurface.

4. How are we doing on

_____?

5. Do we need to change anything?

6. Who will be responsible for which part of our solution that we will do together? For example: " I will be responsible for _____and you have agreed that you will be responsible for _____.

Resolving conflicts in a healthy way can be challenging, especially when you're feeling angry. However, by taking a step back, using "I" statements, actively listening, empathizing with the other person, focusing on the issue, brainstorming solutions together, and agreeing on next steps and your follow-up, you can work toward a solution that promotes understanding and strengthens relationships. Remember that conflicts are a natural part of any relationship and resolving them in a healthy way can lead to greater understanding and deeper connections with those that you are having conflict with.

Healthy relationships are built on effective communication and conflict resolution skills. In order to build and maintain healthy relationships, it's important to use best communication practices in conflict resolution. By doing so, you can build and maintain healthy relationships based on effective communication and mutual understanding. By approaching it with empathy, openness, and a willingness to find a solution, you can build stronger, more resilient relationships.

Chapter 6:

Anger Management in Specific

Contexts

Anger can occur anywhere, but there are certain situations where it's especially important to know how to manage it effectively when it arises in order to mitigate potentially disastrous or permanent consequences.

The Workplace

It's extremely important to manage anger in the workplace. Uncontrolled anger in the workplace can lead to negative consequences such as damaged relationships, decreased productivity, and even job loss. In this section, we'll discuss anger management in the workplace and I'll provide some tips on how to effectively manage anger at work.

Case Study

I once worked with a client ("Frank") who had been working at a prestigious company for several years. Frank was known for his hard work and dedication, and he was well-liked by his coworkers. However, things started to change when a new manager was hired in his department.

The new manager had a different management style than Frank was used to and was often critical, and in particular to Frank's work. He would often give him tasks that were impossible to complete in the given timeframes. Frank did his best to meet the new manager's expectations, but he found himself becoming increasingly stressed and frustrated.

To make matters worse, Frank's coworkers started to notice a change in his behavior. He was quick to snap at them and became easily agitated over small things. They tried to talk to him and offer their support, but Frank was too caught up in his own anger to listen.

As time went on, Frank's behavior became a pattern. He would come into work angry and leave even angrier. He was no longer the hard-working, dedicated employee that everyone knew and admired. Instead, he had become a liability to the company.

One day, after several complaints from coworkers and a string of mistakes made by Frank, his manager called him into his office and expressed his concerns about Frank's behavior and gave him a final warning. He told Frank that if he didn't change his attitude and behavior, he would be fired.

Frank was stunned by this warning. He had never been reprimanded at work before, and he was in disbelief that his behavior had gotten to this point. However, instead of taking the manager's warning to heart and making a change, Frank became even more angry and resentful.

The following week, Frank's anger finally boiled over. He got into a heated argument with a coworker and said things that he immediately regretted. The next day, he was called into the manager's office and told that he was being let go.

Frank was devastated. He had lost his job, and he knew he had himself to blame. He had allowed his anger and frustration to get out of control, and it had cost him everything.

In the end, Frank had learned a valuable lesson about the importance of controlling his anger in the workplace. His behavior had not only affected his own life but also the lives of those around him. It was a harsh wake-up call, but one that he knew he needed to learn from if he ever wanted to succeed in a professional setting again.

Understanding the Causes of Anger in the Workplace

As a mental health practitioner and specialist in DEM (Disruptive Event Management) incidents requiring critical incident debriefing and defusing, I have worked for a company for a number of years that provide specialized services to both the private and government sectors and I have responded to over 150 events in my career, such as mass shootings, workplace violence resulting in suicide and homicide, hostage situations, armed robberies, civil unrest, and next-of-kin notifications for death-related incidents. One of those incidents that I responded to in northern CA involved the shooting death of coworkers on the job and then the shooter taking his own life. The shooter had worked for the USPS for many years and felt that he had been unfairly criticized and overworked for many years despite no reported efforts to inform management of his feelings. Over the course of many years, his coworkers had noticed how his anger had increased and he was often irritable and would lash out at those around him that he felt were treating him unfairly. Sadly, this ended in the taking of the lives of his coworkers as well as his own.

We see this type of incident happening over and over in the increase of mass shootings that the US experiences and with easy access to guns. It is critically important that when anyone sees anger or rage unfolding in someone that they work with that it is reported to management when one sees it arising and never defusing so that the proper interventions can be done to help someone get the kind of mental help they need and to thwart such a tragedy from happening.

The first step in effectively managing anger in the workplace is to understand the underlying causes of anger. In the workplace, anger can be caused by various factors such as:

- **Work overload**

- **Lack of control**

- **Conflicts with coworkers or superiors**

- **Unfair treatment**

- **Lack of or inadequate communication with superiors**

Identifying the cause of your anger can help you manage it in a healthier way. In the earlier case of Frank, it was his experience with a new manager whose management style he didn't like. Recognize your triggers and identify them. This involves being aware of situations that make you feel angry or frustrated. Once you are aware of your triggers, you can develop strategies to manage your anger when these situations arise. For example, if you know that a certain coworker always pushes your hot buttons, you can prepare yourself mentally before interacting with them.

Are there any triggers for you at your workplace and what are they?

_____

_____

_____

_____

_____

_____

_____

What will be your solutions to them?

_____

_____

_____

_____

_____

_____

_____

Managing Your Anger in the Workplace

Below are some tips and techniques to help you manage your anger in the workplace:

- **Practice deep breathing and relaxation techniques**

  Deep breathing and relaxation techniques can help you manage your anger in the workplace. When you feel angry or frustrated, take a few deep breaths and focus on your breathing. You can also practice relaxation techniques such as meditation or yoga during your breaks to help you manage stress and prevent anger from building up.

- **Use assertive communication**

  Assertive communication involves expressing your thoughts and feelings in a clear and direct manner, while respecting the thoughts and feelings of others. Using assertive communication can help you manage conflicts in the workplace and prevent anger from escalating. When communicating with coworkers or superiors, focus on the issue at hand and avoid making personal attacks.

  What will you use as an assertive way of communicating your needs when it comes to your triggers at work?

- **Take a break**

  If you feel yourself becoming angry or frustrated, can you take a break? Go for a walk? Get a cup of tea or coffee? Do something else that will help you relax and take your mind off the situation? Engage in a mindfulness exercise? Taking a break can help you calm down and gain a fresh perspective on the situation.

  What will you do on your break at work to help yourself?

  _____
  _____
  _____
  _____
  _____
  _____
  _____
  _____

- **Seek support**

  If you are struggling to manage your anger in the workplace, it is important to seek support. This can involve talking to a coworker, supervisor, or a human resources representative in your HR department about your concerns. You can also seek support from an EAP (Employee Assistance Professional) therapist or counselor who specializes in anger management at your workplace. Most companies either employ them on site or provide access to them through your health insurance. Seeking support can help you manage your anger in a healthier way and prevent negative consequences.

  Anger management in the workplace is an important skill that can help you manage stress, prevent conflicts, and maintain positive relationships with coworkers and superiors. By understanding the causes of anger, recognizing your triggers, practicing deep breathing and relaxation techniques, using assertive communication, taking breaks, setting boundaries, and seeking support, you can effectively create a positive work environment. Remember that anger is a natural emotion, and it's okay to feel angry at times. However, by managing your anger in a healthy way, you can prevent negative consequences and build stronger, more positive relationships with those around you.

- **Set boundaries**

   Setting boundaries is an important part of managing anger in the workplace. This involves establishing clear boundaries around your work and personal life. For example, if you are constantly checking emails or taking work calls during your personal time, you may feel "used," overwhelmed, and stressed, which can lead to anger. By setting clear boundaries, you can manage your workload and prevent stress from building up. It is important to speak to your management or HR department when you feel that your personal time is being taken unfairly.

   Which of your workplace boundaries are being crossed?

   _____

   _____

   _____

   _____

   _____

   _____

   _____

   _____

   What will you say and do to express the need for your boundary?

   _____

   _____

   _____

_____

_____

_____

_____

_____

- **More Tips on Setting Boundaries in the Workplace**

   Having healthy boundaries in the workplace is essential and it involves setting limits on what is acceptable and unacceptable behavior from yourself and others, and creates a sense of safety and respect in the workplace. Healthy boundaries can help to reduce the likelihood of conflict and anger arising, as well as helping you to maintain your own well-being and productivity. By defining your boundaries, communicating them clearly to those that you work with, enforcing them, practicing self-care, and seeking support, you can create a safe and respectful work environment that supports you.

   Here are some strategies for you:

1. **Define your boundaries:** Before you can set healthy boundaries, you need to know what they are. Take some time to reflect on what you need from your work environment in terms of respect, communication, workload, and other factors. Identify the areas where you feel your boundaries have been crossed or where you feel uncomfortable and determine what changes you would like to see.

   Is there anything that you need to convey to others at work that you haven't done already?

   _____

   _____

   _____

   _____

   _____

   _____

_____
_____
_____

When will you convey what you need? (Today, tomorrow, this week, next week?)

_____
_____

2. **Communicate clearly:** Once you have defined your boundaries, it is important to communicate them clearly to others. Don't forget to use your "I" statements to express how you feel and what you need, rather than blaming or attacking others. Be specific about what behaviors are and are not acceptable to you and explain the consequences of crossing your boundaries if your coworkers cross them.

3. **Enforce your boundaries:** Setting boundaries is not enough; you also need to enforce them. This means saying "no" when you need to, standing up for yourself when your boundaries are crossed, and following through on consequences if necessary. Remember that boundaries are only effective if they are consistently maintained.

How will you enforce your boundaries? (For example: "The next time you ask me to take on work when it is my own personal time, I want you to know that I am going to say 'No' to you.).

_____
_____
_____
_____
_____
_____
_____
_____

4. **Practice self-care:** Taking care of yourself is an essential part of setting healthy boundaries. Make sure you are getting enough rest, exercise, and nutritious food, and take breaks when you need them. This can help you to maintain your emotional resilience and prevent burnout.

In what ways are you going to practice self-care?

_____

_____

_____

_____

_____

_____

_____

_____

_____

5. **Seek support:** Dealing with anger management in the workplace can be challenging, and it is important to seek support when you need it. Talk to trusted colleagues or friends outside of work, or consider speaking to a mental health practitioner. They can provide guidance and help you develop strategies for maintaining healthy boundaries and managing your anger effectively.

Anger Management in Relationships and Family Settings

Managing anger in relationships and family settings can be particularly challenging, as these environments can be highly emotional and personal. However, it is important to develop effective anger management strategies to maintain healthy relationships and prevent conflict from escalating. Here are some tips for managing anger in relationships and family settings:

1. **Recognize your triggers:** What are they and with whom?

_____

_____

_____

_____

_____

_____

2. **Practice active listening:** It is important to listen as well as speak. Fully engage yourself with what the other person is saying, without interrupting or thinking about your response.

3. **Use your "I" statements:** Don't resort to using "You always do this... You always do that" statements. Instead, use "I" statements, such as "I feel upset when ____ starts to happen." Avoid blame, which creates an air of defensiveness, and instead encourage understanding and empathy.

4. **Take a time-out:** A time-out can be an effective way to cool down and prevent conflict from escalating. Calm down before returning to the conversation.

5. **Develop problem-solving skills:** Approach the problem in a constructive way. Practice problem-solving skills by identifying the issue, brainstorming solutions, and evaluating the pros and cons of each. This can help to find a mutually acceptable solution and prevent future conflicts.

6. **Seek outside help:** If managing anger in relationships and family settings is particularly challenging, it may be helpful to seek outside help. It is also a safety net for all involved.

In addition to these tips, it is important to remember that managing anger in relationships and family settings is an ongoing process that requires practice and patience. It is important to approach these situations with empathy, understanding, and a willingness to listen and learn.

Anger in Terms of Children and Adolescents

Getting angry is a normal human emotion, but it can lead to negative consequences, especially when dealing with children and adolescents. It is important for parents, caregivers, and educators to understand the risks associated with uncontrolled anger and develop effective anger management strategies when communicating with children and adolescents. In addition, it is crucial to recognize the dangers of engaging in child abuse when anger is at its extreme.

The effects of anger on children and adolescents can be significant. Uncontrolled anger can lead to emotional and behavioral problems in children, including anxiety, depression, and aggression. This can lead to problems at school, with friends, and at home. Children may become withdrawn or act out in response to anger, leading to further conflict and stress.

When communicating with children and adolescents, it is important to remain calm and avoid becoming angry or aggressive. Use a calm and reassuring tone of voice, and be patient and understanding when listening to their concerns. Avoid using criticism or blame, as this can lead to feelings of shame or guilt. Instead, focus on positive reinforcement and offer praise for good behavior.

It is also important to model healthy anger management techniques, such as taking deep breaths or counting to ten when feeling angry. Encourage children and adolescents to express their anger in healthy ways, such as through art or exercise. This can help them to develop positive coping mechanisms and reduce the risk of emotional or behavioral problems.

It is crucial to recognize the dangers of engaging in child abuse when anger is at its extreme. Child abuse is never an acceptable response to anger or frustration and can have serious long-term consequences for the child's mental and physical health. It is important to seek help if you find yourself struggling with anger and the risk of abusive behavior with your children.

If you are having trouble managing your anger, seek professional help from a therapist or counselor. It is important to recognize the risks associated with uncontrolled anger when dealing with children and adolescents. Developing effective anger management strategies and modeling healthy behavior can help to reduce the risk of negative consequences for children and adolescents. It is crucial to seek help if you find yourself struggling with anger and the risk of abusive behavior, as this can have serious consequences for both you and your child. Remember, healthy communication and positive reinforcement can go a long way in maintaining a healthy and positive relationship with children.

Domestic Violence

Domestic violence, also known as intimate partner violence, is a pattern of behavior used by one partner to gain power and control over the other in a romantic relationship. While anger can be a contributing factor in domestic violence, it is important to note that not all anger leads to violence and not all violence is caused by anger. Domestic violence can take many forms, including verbal, emotional, and physical abuse, and can range from mild to severe.

Verbal violence refers to the use of words to intimidate, degrade, or threaten a partner. This can include shouting, name-calling, insults, and put-downs. Verbal violence can also include gaslighting, where a partner manipulates the other's perception of reality, causing them to doubt their own thoughts and feelings.

Emotional abuse involves manipulating a partner's emotions and behaviors through tactics such as isolation, intimidation, and coercion. Emotional abuse can include things like controlling a partner's finances, preventing them from seeing friends or family, or using guilt or shame to manipulate their behavior.

Physical abuse is the use of physical force to harm or control a partner. This can include hitting, slapping, kicking, pushing, and other forms of physical violence. Physical abuse can also involve the use of weapons or objects to inflict harm.

It is important to note that domestic violence can involve a combination of verbal, emotional, and physical abuse, and can vary in severity. Any form of domestic violence, regardless of its severity, can have serious and long-lasting consequences for the victim, including physical injury, emotional trauma, and in extreme cases, death.

Warranted, the term "domestic violence" typically involves a pattern of abusive behavior rather than a single incident, but it can also include a one-time catastrophic event that results in homicide. The severity and frequency of the abusive behavior also plays a role in determining whether a situation constitutes domestic violence. For example, a single instance of verbal violence may not necessarily constitute domestic violence, but a protracted pattern of verbal, emotional, or physical abuse over a prolonged period of time would.

Have a Safety Plan

If you are involved in a domestic violence situation and you or your partner is not willing to change abusive behavior, it is important to have a safety plan in place. A safety plan is a personalized, practical plan that outlines steps one can take to protect yourself and your children from violence or abuse.

Here are some steps to consider when developing a safety plan:

1. **Create a support network:** Reach out to family, friends, and professionals who can provide you with emotional support and assistance in leaving the relationship.

    Who is your support network?

    _____

    _____

    _____

    _____

    _____

_____

_____

2. **Keep important documents safe:** Keep copies of important documents such as identification, birth certificates, social security cards, and financial records in a safe place, outside of the home if possible.

   Where are your important documents and what are they?

   _____

   _____

   _____

   _____

   _____

   _____

   _____

3. **Plan for an emergency:** Have a bag packed with essential items such as clothing, money, medication, and a cell phone charger in case you need to leave in a hurry.

   Where do you keep the to-go bag and what is in it?

   _____

   _____

   _____

   _____

   _____

   _____

   _____

4. **Have a safe place to go:** Identify a safe place to go in case you need to leave your home quickly, such as a friend's house, shelter, or hotel.

Where will that safe have be and what is the address and phone number?

_____

_____

_____

_____

_____

_____

_____

_____

5. **Develop a code word or signal:** Develop a code word or signal with a trusted friend or family member that can indicate when you need help or support.

   What is the signal or code word that you would use when you need it?

   _____

   _____

   _____

   _____

   _____

   _____

6. **Consider obtaining a restraining order:** A restraining order can legally require your abuser to stay away from you, your home, and your workplace.

   What are the steps I need to do in order to get a restraining order?

   _____

   _____

   _____

   _____

_____

_____

_____

7. **Contact domestic violence organizations:** Domestic violence organizations can provide you with resources, support, and guidance on leaving a violent relationship.

   Where is the nearest domestic violence shelter to me? Phone number and address?

   _____

   _____

   _____

   _____

   _____

   _____

   _____

8. **Keep a low social profile:** Refrain from posting anything on social media.

9. **Time appropriately:** Plan when you will leave and ensure that it is a safe time for you to leave.

10. **Call for help:** Call 911 for emergency assistance or for a police escort to assist you when you leave your home.

Always prioritize your safety and the safety of your children. A safety plan can help you take steps to protect yourself and move toward a safer future.

It is important to seek help if you or someone you know is experiencing domestic violence. This can include reaching out to a trusted friend or family member, seeking support from a therapist or counselor, or contacting a domestic violence hotline or shelter. It is important to remember that domestic violence is never the fault of the victim and that there is help and support available for those who are experiencing it.

Remember that leaving an abusive partner can be extremely dangerous, so it's essential to have a plan in place and reach out for help. You don't have to go through this alone. There are resources and support available to help you.

When Children Are Involved

When anger is not managed properly, it can lead to negative consequences, especially when dealing with children. In addition, it is crucial to recognize the dangers of engaging in child abuse when anger is at its extreme.

Legal consequences are usually the outcome, with your local Child Protective Services and law enforcement often intervening on the behalf of the protection and best interests of the child. It is important to seek help if you find yourself struggling with anger and the risk of abusive behavior toward your children. They can provide guidance and support.

The Financial and Social Impacts of Anger

While there is no specific data on the financial toll of out-of-control anger and rage on US society, it's clear that incidents of assault and battery can have significant costs for taxpayers. The costs associated with legal resources and incarceration for individuals who are arrested for violent crimes are substantial.

According to the National Institute of Justice, the average cost of incarcerating an inmate in the United States is approximately $31,286 per year. This means that the cost of incarcerating a single individual for just one year can be significant, and the costs can add up quickly for individuals who are sentenced to longer periods of time.

In addition to the costs of incarceration, there are also significant costs associated with legal resources such as police investigations, court proceedings, and public defenders. These costs can vary depending on the severity of the crime, the length of the trial, and other factors.

It is worth noting that the financial toll of out-of-control anger and rage is not just limited to the costs associated with incarceration and legal resources. There can also be significant costs associated with medical treatment for victims of violent crimes, lost productivity for individuals who are injured or murdered as a result of violent crime, and other indirect costs.

Overall, while it is difficult to estimate the exact financial toll of out-of-control anger and rage on US society, it's clear that there are significant costs associated with violent crime, and these costs are borne by taxpayers in many different ways.

Firstly, taxpayers may have to pay for the costs of prosecuting and convicting the individuals who committed the assault or assault and battery. This can include costs associated with hiring lawyers, court fees, and other expenses related to the legal process.

Once the individual is convicted and sent to prison, taxpayers will also have to pay for the cost of incarceration. This includes the cost of providing food, clothing, and shelter for the prisoner, as well as medical care and other necessary services. In addition, prisons may also require additional security measures to prevent further incidents of violence, which can add to the overall cost.

If the prisoner is serving a long sentence, taxpayers may have to pay for these costs for many years. This can put a significant strain on state and federal budgets, as well as on taxpayers themselves.

Furthermore, taxpayers may also be impacted indirectly by the cost of incarcerating individuals, as incarceration can have a significant impact on the families of prisoners, as well as on their communities. This can lead to increased social and economic problems, such as higher rates of poverty and unemployment, which can ultimately be costly for taxpayers to address.

Overall, the costs associated with incarcerating prisoners who have committed assault and assault and battery can be substantial.

Conclusion

So let's recap the vital points that you have discovered in *Anger Management, Taming the Dragon Within*:

1. You now understand the physiology of anger and that it is a natural response of your body to perceived or real threats.

2. You can identify personal triggers and the coping skills needed to manage them effectively. The most common triggers include stress, frustration, and feeling powerless.

3. You have uncovered coping strategies that you can employ such as physical activities, relaxation techniques, and cognitive-behavioral strategies. These strategies can help in managing the physical and mental symptoms of anger.

4. You have come to understand what CBT (Cognitive Behavioral Therapy) is and how important it is to change the way we think and behave when we feel angry. Techniques include identifying and challenging negative or distorted thoughts and changing them in the moment they surface to positive ones, in order to achieve positive outcomes. It takes time and practice.

5. You have mastered how to effectively communicate your anger or frustration with others in healthy ways through conflict resolution.

6. You can analyze anger management in specific contexts such as in the workplace and develop healthy boundaries that you can use at work as well as with friends and family.

7. You recognize the dangers of uncontrolled anger and how it can lead to child abuse and domestic violence, and the legal and financial implications that go along with that type of behavior,

leading to serious long-term consequences for both the perpetrator and the victim's mental and physical health.

8. You have come a long way on this self-anger management journey, and I hope you find value in your guidebook and let it continue to be a great resource for you whenever you need to access it, or just to refresh the information that you have just discovered for yourself!

A Final Note

I want to thank you for taking the time to read this book. It is my hope that you have gained information that you can begin to apply in your daily lives that will result in your life's enrichment as well as for those you know and love.

I want to encourage you that with patience, practice, and persistence, it is possible to learn how to manage anger effectively and maintain healthy relationships.

So, in conclusion, now is the time to welcome yourself to a new you, now that you have discovered that you can be in control of your anger! A job well done!

Call to Action

If you have found this book helpful and would like others to know about it, if you would be so kind as to take the time to review this book on Amazon.com, my family and I would greatly appreciate it!

Mackenzie Skye, Ph.D., LMFT

References

Bloxham, G. (2017). *Anger Management: Understanding Anger and Finding the Right Way to Deal With It*. Marcasa Books.

Hanh, T.N. (2002). *Anger: Wisdom for Cooling the Flames*. Riverhead Books.

Karmin, A. (2016). *Anger Management Workbook for Men: Take Control of Your Anger and Master Your Emotions*. Althea Press.

Lerner, H. (2014). *The Dance of Anger: A Woman's Guide to Changing the Patterns of Intimate Relationships*. William Morrow Paperbacks.

McLaren, K. (2010). *The Language of Emotions: What Your Feelings Are Trying to Tell You*. Sounds True Publishing.

*Morin, A. How to Control Your Anger: 25 Tips to Manage Your Temper and Emotions.

Nay, R.W. (2014). *The Anger Management Workbook: Use the STOP Method to Replace Destructive Responses With Constructive Behavior*. Guilford Press.

Nay, R.W. (2010). *Overcoming Anger in Your Relationship: How to Break the Cycle of Arguments, Put-Downs, and Stony Silences*. Guilford Press.

*Scott, E. Anger Management Techniques That Actually Work.

*Tartakovsky, M. 10 Tips to Help You Deal With Anger and Frustration. PsychCentral.com.

*Segal, J. The Power of Apology in Anger Management.

Made in the USA
Middletown, DE
13 January 2025

68757076R00046